# SOMNIO

## The Way We See It

**TIFFANY** ADAIR
**PUSHPA** RAJ ACHARYA
**SHARMILA** POKHAREL
**YUKARI** MELDRUM

The TiPSY Press©

The **TiPSY** Press[©]
Copyright © 2015 Tiffany Adair, Pushpa Raj Acharya, Sharmila Pokharel, and Yukari Meldrum.


Library and Archives Canada Cataloguing in Publication

Cataloguing in Publication (CIP) data available at the Library and Archives Canada website (collectionscanada.gc.ca) and at **TiPSY**press.com

ISBN 978–0–9947301–0–7 (pbk.)
ISBN 978–0–9947301–0–7 (e-book)
First Edition

Book design by Zach Hoskin (zachhoskin.com)
Edited and proofread by Ellen Kartz
Printed and bound in Canada by Scan Copy Print Inc.

Published by The **TiPSY** Press[©]
P.O. Box 2108
Edmonton, AB T5J 2P4
**TiPSY**press.com

The TiPSY Press gratefully acknowledges the support of the Edmonton Arts Council through the Cultural Diversity in the Arts Project Grant.

# TABLE *of* CONTENTS

## POEMS *and* ILLUSTRATIONS

## PUSHPA RAJ ACHARYA

# The White Wolf

Pushpa Raj Acharya

My friend
one snowy evening
we saw your furry whiteness
near our home.
I was playing with my older sister.

Was it mere chance, an innocent stray,
a plan? You were rare here.

We hailed you—howling. You
gazed at us flicking your ears.
Our mother came out, her
eyes wide.

Would you have played with us?

In my drawing sessions at school, I
saw you again
and many times. I looked at you
right into the glow of your eyes.

Was there an imprint in your mind, too,
of two kids trying to communicate
in a strange accent? Or a child's fixed gaze?

My mother thought that I
was scared. The reason I saw you
in my room at nights was not fear.

After many winters, I can now afford
to visit the north. A package tour
for boxed people
in downtown apartments!

Today, I intend to slip away
from the tour choreography
to meet the Great White Wolf. My dear friend,
we will stand face-to-face and gaze at each other
under the cold moonlight
whirling from the sky.

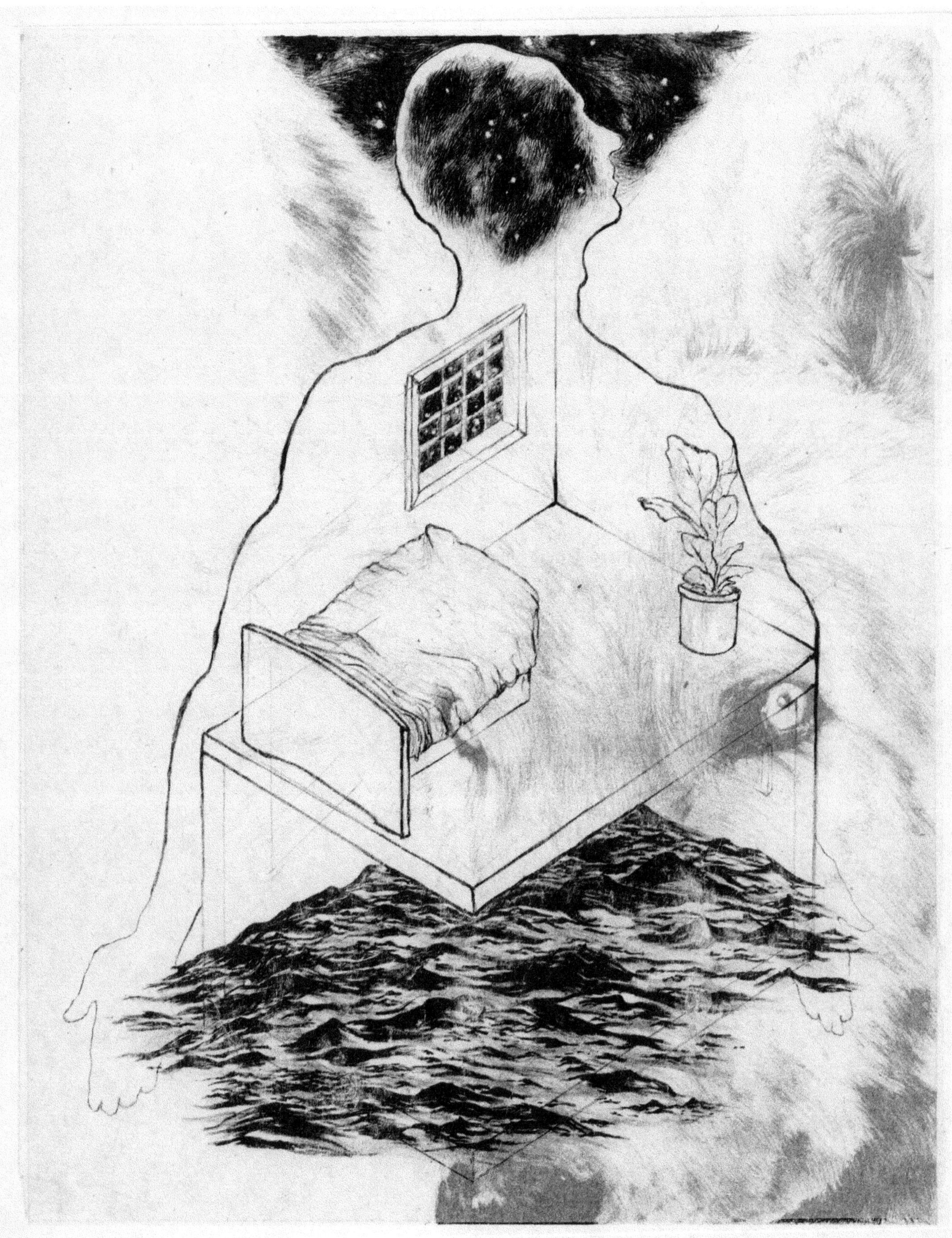

**White Wolf** Tiffany Adair
Lithograph, chine collé
2015

# A Night
Pushpa Raj Acharya

From the depths of a night arises a cry
a wild goose's agony from a lake nearby

A farmer's little daughter pities his fate
in a bamboo hut, she's pensive this late

She imagines the flight of a dragonfly
born out of the dancing rays of the clear sky

The waves of light dissolve the lake
and the anguish of being awake

# Spring
Pushpa Raj Acharya


An evening in April.

I go for a walk with S— and W—
We are on the high-level bridge
between the city and the university.
The chilling wind blows on our noses.

We stop and look below us.
The river has reappeared
cracking open
the grip of ice and snow.


Another evening in May.

It showers.
We see from the bridge
how the city lights enter the raindrops
and plunge into the river.


We dream of sailing in canoes.

Winter's compassion is time.

# Control
Pushpa Raj Acharya


Lying on the warm sand, I
watch the surf from the Pacific roll ceaselessly.

In the turmoil of an unstable ocean,
infinite justice swims like a cod
and spreads everywhere. To the skyline. To
the city.

Men have always wanted
to control the cities. Perfect their machinery. Find
an impeccable precision. Invent laws, and even crimes.

I control nothing. I
live like a moose, or a loon, or a bear.

I'm lying on the warm sand.

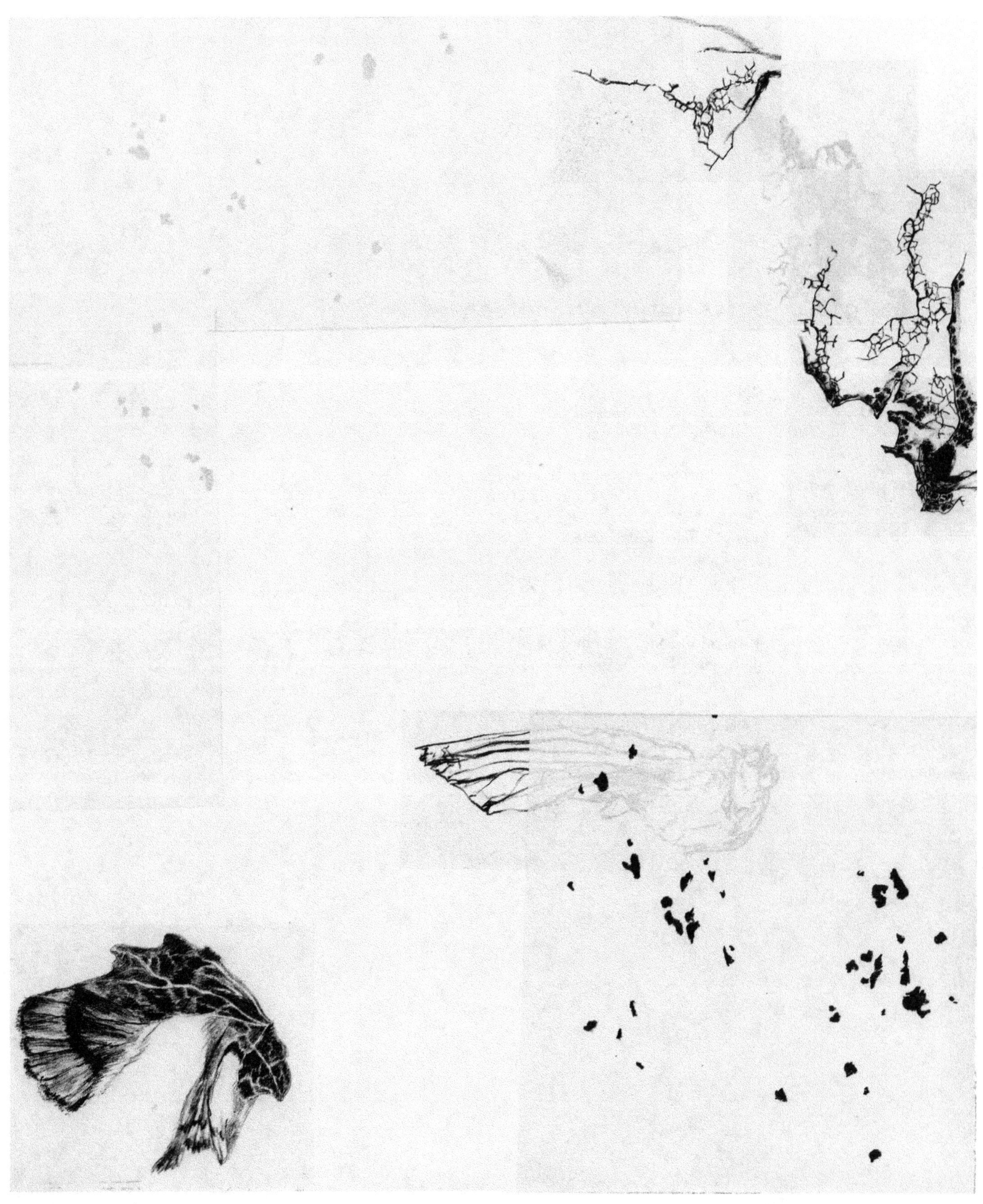

**Control** Tiffany Adair
Lithograph, chine collé
2015

# First Autumn in Edmonton

Pushpa Raj Acharya

"Magpies are so ugly:
See, they've  yellow beaks,
'n they're always hungry!"

My old professor does not like them much,
but always gives them morsels of bread.

Later, when I walk home,
I see magpies
sitting on the branches and breathing fire.

The green leaves
turn yellow, they fall, they go dry.
The bright branches become
pale, naked, stiff.

Sometimes beyond the tree lines,
I notice the blazing sky of the west.

# Forgiving
Pushpa Raj Acharya

1.

The rain falling from the clouds
forgives all:

it touches your body from above,
flows down to your eyes, face, lips,
washes through your body,
drops from fingers, toes, heels.

Stand still in the rain,
close your eyes,
imagine your body is now a tree—
witness the art of forgiving.

2.

The rays spreading from the sun
forgive all:

they touch your body all at once,
the body absorbs them,
it tingles as if the warm sand under feet
has sent the rays back to belly, chest, head.

Stand still in the sun,
close your eyes,
imagine as if your body is now a tree—
witness the art of forgiving.

3.

Then—
let go!

---

# 許し
プスパ・アチャリヤ
翻訳：メルドラム由香理
Japanese Translation by
Yukari Meldrum

1.

雲から舞い降りる雨は
全てを許す

それは上から身体に触れ、
目、顔、唇をつたわり、
全身を洗い、
手の指、足の指、かかとから流れ落ちる。

雨の中に静かに立ち、
目を閉じ、
身体が木であるかのように
許しという芸術を見つめよ。

2.

太陽からひろがる光線は
全てを許す

身体の全てに一度に触れ、
身体に吸収され、うずく
足の下のあたたかい砂に反射し
腹部、胸部、頭部に輝きが届くように。

日光の中に静かに立ち、
目を閉じて、
身体が木であるかのように
ゆるしという芸術を見つめよ。

3.

そして、
解き放て！

# The Other Shore
Pushpa Raj Acharya

We are sailing on,
we are sailing on.

The world is a river
and the rings of memories slip from our fingers
into its watery depths.

The rings are hidden
in the belly of the river.
Will the loved ones forget those
whom they love?
Will the currents throw the treasures back?

I think of a woman—
one half a nymph, the other half a sage.
She had found hope
on the other shore.

**The Other Shore** Tiffany Adair
Lithograph, chine collé
2015

# Walking
Pushpa Raj Acharya

I've fallen in love with walking. It has
wondrous colors.

Profound red and orphic dark. Between
them wavers my body.

A blue curve of smile,
the white waves of rush,
the green sway of tallness.
Red, brown, black soil. Foliage and earth.

The silver gray and hexing tan.
I see the moon—
a fine, big, bewitching charm.

I'm a different man.

# Sand and Snow
Pushpa Raj Acharya


All things are on a continuum
from the Taklamakan to the Arctic.

The silence of winter gyrates
once as an eternal sorrow of the earth
where all goes into oblivion,

then, as a one-night blossom
which grows out of the forgetfulness of dry soil.

Metaphors are the extended arms of the sun.

So, words fall like rain on petals,
words fall like light on leaves,
words rise like sand in wind,
words ebb like the moon in seas.

All things are on a continuum.
The inside-out of words, the outside-in of senses,
the silent cries of sand and snow,
all disseminate from the spinning core of the earth.

# The Strings

Pushpa Raj Acharya

Come, come,
listen to the sound of the strings.

One day Oneness will
quilt you and grass. A tree and a sparrow.

The sound of the strings is
a reminder. Like a river that seams rain and sea.

Lightning writes on the clouds
the notes of dissonance. Thunderous.

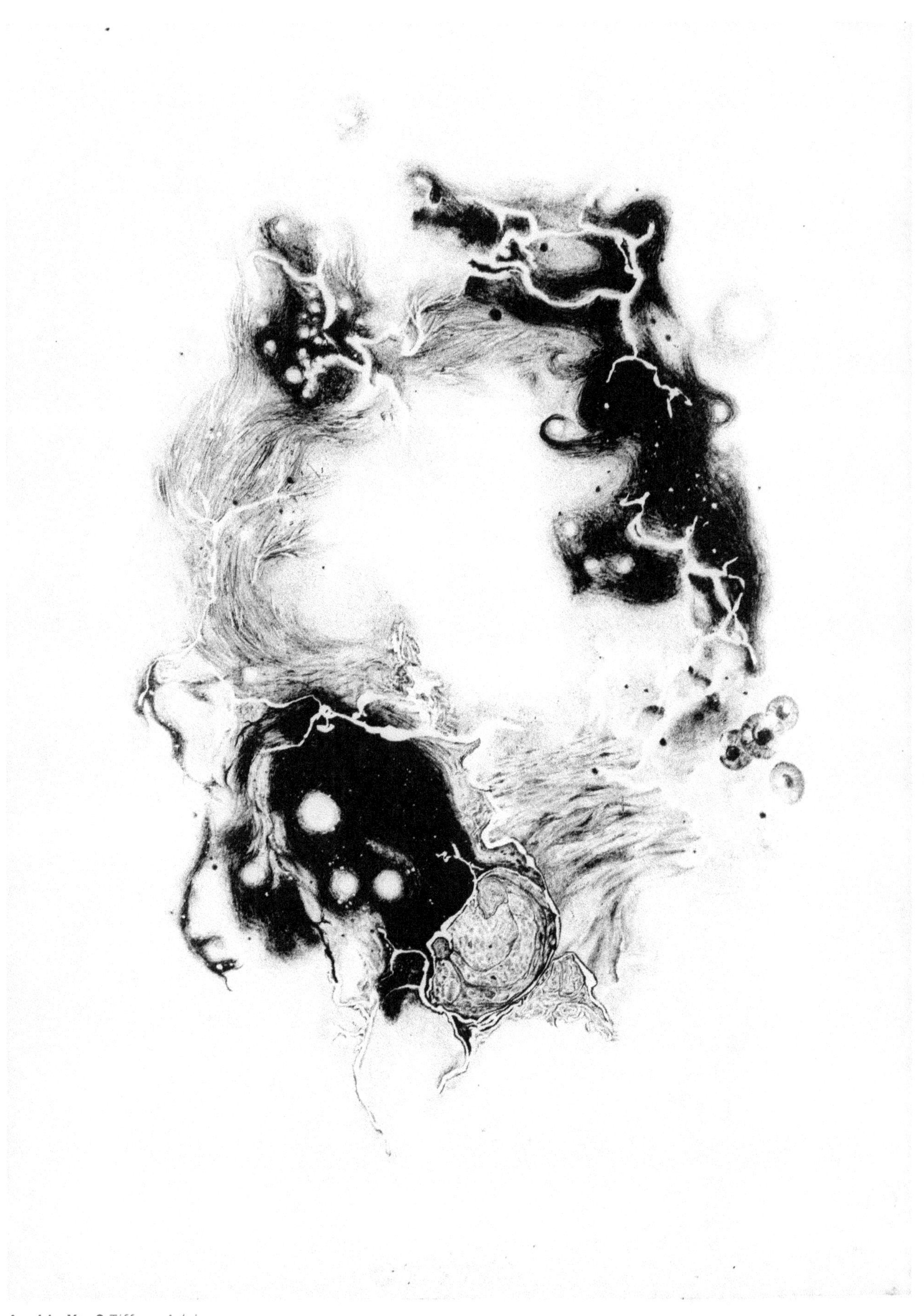

**Am I In You?** Tiffany Adair
Lithograph
2015

# SHARMILA POKHAREL

# Fear of English
Sharmila Pokharel

My dear friend,
how fluently you speak English!
I'm as eloquent in *Nepali*.

For me,
English has always been a python.
At school, when the English teacher
appeared in front of me,
my lips and mouth would go dry.

Big eyes, long beard,
a huge stick in his hand,
the English teacher,
the strictest person in the world
and the English he taught
sounded treacherous.

When I was ten,
a nine-and-a-half-years-old Anju
showed me a tangled thing: **&**
I had never seen it before.
In front of my relatives,
she asked, ***Do you know what it is?***
It surely was a snake, I thought.

As I started learning *A*,*B*,*C*,*D*,
English was the cobra swallowing everything.
***Thank you very much!***
***No problem at all!***

I could not go
beyond these expressions.
Neither could I scold in English
as spontaneously as you did.

Thank God
I don't need English
to cry or laugh.

# Green Plants
Sharmila Pokharel


The human trails
where else could they reach?
Cities, towns, villages, jungles
oceans and deserts

Where else could they
be wandering every time?
Where else could I be,
searching for myself nowadays?

A piece of land
a beautiful house
a garden full of flowers
a small family
all these necessities
were there
where I resided before I left

With green plants and flowers
in pots within the house,
I amuse myself and think:
there was greenery everywhere
in the place which I abandoned
and never could there be snow
and never could my garden be dead

Somewhere in the corner
of that village
was the hut of a
poor young girl called - *Sani*

A small front yard
painted with cow dung
little flower garden
full of roses and lilies

# An Immigrant Mind
Sharmila Pokharel

Everyday
it's the same me
who takes the train
but with different feelings

In the long winter months
when snow makes me
shiver all the time
I ask myself
whose country is this?
I say, I have mine
beyond the skyline

On short summer days,
when leaves come out on the trees
and rain makes the land look beautiful,
all the roads look heavenly
and I shout out loud, "I love Canada"

Years have passed
I take the same train
with different emotions
in different seasons

My immigrant mind
lives in two countries
side by side

# 移民の心
サーミラ・ポカレル
翻訳：メルドラム由香理
Japanese Translation by Yukari Meldrum

まいにち
同じ自分が
電車に乗る
違う気分で

雪が降る
長い冬の日々
いつも寒さにふるえ
自問する
この国は誰のものなのか、と
地平線より遠くに
わたしの国がある

短い夏の日々
木々に葉が萌える時
地面が雨で美しくなる時
全ての道路が神々しく
わたしはカナダが大好きだと叫ぶ

年月が過ぎ去り
同じ電車に乗る
ちがう気持ちで
ちがう季節に

わたしの移民の心は
二つの国に
隣同士

# Far from the Skyline

Sharmila Pokharel

Like an old melody still in memory,
as a secret story inside the heart,
the bamboo trees in my backyard,
the mango trees in my front yard.

The land that grows
thousands of papayas and *lichis*,
the soil that flourishes marigolds and lilies.

O, my childhood land,
if I come back
will you still embrace me
as you did before?

Do you still have
the giant *simal* tree
on the roadside?

Do you still carry
the smell of jasmine flowers
all over the village?

# To My Child
Sharmila Pokharel

My dear,
wait in the cozy fluid of the womb
kick or sleep as much as you want
but don't come to the world yet.

It is not ready for you.
Bone-breaking chilly winter,
heart-breaking sad news,
surround everything right now.

Your eyes are still too small
to witness such horrifying things.
Wait until this Earth is filled
with love and compassion again.

Summer will come soon.
Wait until trees cover with leaves,
birds start singing,
flowers begin blossoming again.

# Mother
Sharmila Pokharel

If I go home
I will find my mother
doing the household chores,
tears rolling down her cheeks

With the dream of earning more
I am rushing on and on
towards success
counting each second and each minute

While she cleans the same dishes,
prepares one meal after another,
cleans again and counts the days again

As the mornings, afternoons, and evenings pass by,
her body stoops a little more
her eyes get blurred a little more

# The Face Not in Facebook
Sharmila Pokharel

When I smiled,
there was nobody to click my photo
so I smiled the way I liked.
Otherwise I had to say *cheese* and hide
my uneven teeth behind my lips.

Nowadays, they say
life has become like a high-speed train,
but my life is still a bullock-cart,
which moves but without hurry.

Why should I pace my life like a train
and forget to pick up the tomatoes in my backyard,
and miss the view of the butterflies over the lilies,
and not cook the fresh mustard greens for dinner tonight?

Let my life crawl at its own pace.

**Facebook** Tiffany Adair
Lithograph, chine collé, silkscreen
2015

# When You Arrive
Sharmila Pokharel

Death,
when you arrive
like a child in front of a tiger
weak and breathless
one has to go with you

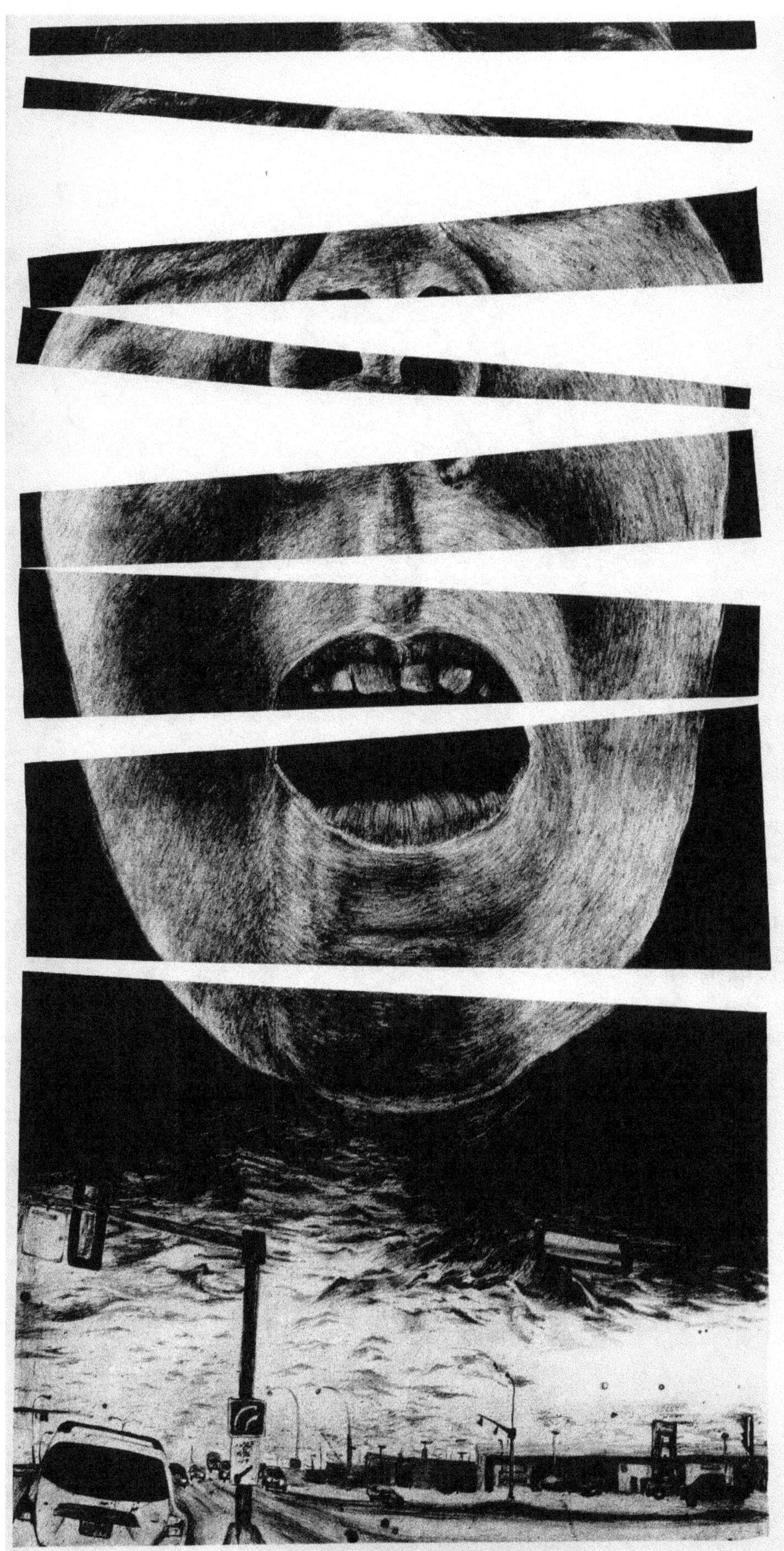

**Breathe** Tiffany Adair
Lithograph, chine collé
2015

# The Battle
Sharmila Pokharel

Yesterday
you were there
so sad

You denied to surrender
I refused to give up
the rule of the game was
one had to lose

Yesterday
neither did you win
nor I kissed the victory

In the journey of ego
neither you reached your destination
nor I arrived at mine

Yesterday, today, and forever,
we keep wasting centuries
in this battle for self

**The Battle** Tiffany Adair
Lithograph
2015

# Run
Sharmila Pokharel


For some reason,
she was addicted to running.
Her feet could not take a break.

One dream, one run
and one achievement
followed by many more!

Not sure why she has
to keep on running
to catch the colourful butterfly
of life.

If someone had told her,
*Stop and breathe &*
*be slow and steady,*
she would have walked
one foot after another
pace to pace — breath to breath
happily, thereafter.

**Run** Tiffany Adair
Lithograph
2015

## YUKARI MELDRUM

# One Day in Winter

Yukari Meldrum

A purring cat,
fuzzy and warm,
snuggled against me.

The sun is low,
illuminating the entire room
through the south window.

It's almost lunch time now.
Everyone must be getting ready
to leave for a mid-day break
from their mindless deskwork.

I am home
enjoying the warmth
of the cat and sunshine
on this large sofa
with a cup of hot tea and a book.

For the first time
in such a long while,
I feel alive.

The fever and aches
from this flu
now somewhat tolerable.

# जाडोको एक दिन

युकारी मेलड्रम

अनुवादः शर्मिला पोखरेल
Nepali Translation by
Sharmila Pokharel

मुलायम र न्यानो बिरालो
म्याउँ म्याउँ गर्दै
घुस्रिरहेको छ मसँगै

अस्ताउँदो सुर्यको किरण
दक्षिणको झ्यालबाट छिरेर
पुरै कोठा उज्यालो पारेको छ

यतिबेला दिउँसोको खाजा खाने समय
सबै जना तैयार हुँदैहुन्
मध्यदिनसम्मको काम सकेर

म आफ्नो निवासमा
यो ठूलो सोफामा
तातो चिया र किताबका साथमा
बिरालो र घामको न्यानोको
आनन्द लिइरहेकोछु

पहिलोपल्ट आज
धेरै धेरै समयपछि
जीवन्त भएकीछु

यो रूघाको ज्वरो र दुखाइ
अब केही मात्रामा
सहन सकिने भएकोछ

# A Life of a Japanese Woman – Early Twentieth Century

Yukari Meldrum

I have just turned twenty years old
and married a man who runs a store—
his family on the wealthy side.

My mom and dad thought
I would be happy
to marry into a rich family.
So I thought…

My husband spends his earnings drinking,
making me plead for money from my parents
so we can have food on our table.
He has two women outside
and gave me a disease I did not deserve.

This is a woman's life.
It's just the way it is.
There is no choice to leave,
for a divorce means being kicked out,
never to see my precious baby—
never, ever again.

My little girl, just eight months old,
strapped onto my back with a pink silk sash,
cries and cries hysterically—
as if she sees my sadness
as if she feels her misery
when she too will be married.

# एक जापानी नारीको जीवन – बीसौं शताब्दीको सुरूतिर

युकारी मेलड्रम

अनुवादः पुष्पराज आचार्य
Nepali translation by
Pushpa Raj Acharya

बीस वर्ष लागेकी छु भर्खर
र बिहे भएको छ पसल गर्ने केटासँग—
उसको परिवार अलि पैसावाल ।

धनी घरमा बिहे भई
म खुशी रहुँला भन्ठाने
मेरा आमाबाबैले ।
मलाई नि त्यस्तै लाग्यो . . .

मेरा स्वामीराजै जाँड धोकी उडाउँछन् कमाइ,
घरमा चूलो बाल्ने पैसा माग्न
माइती पठाउँछन् मलाई ।
बाहिर राखेका छन् दुईओटी रखौटी
बेफ्चाँकमै मलाई सारै नलाग्नुपर्ने रोग ।

यो आइमाईको जुनी मेरो ।
यहाँ चलन पनि यस्तै छ ।
फुत्किभाग्नै पनि रोज्ने बाटो छैन,
पारपाचुके भनेको यहाँ घरनिकाला हो
मेरी रत्न, मेरी नानी फेरि भेट्नै नपाउने गरी—
कहिल्यै भेट्न नपाउने गरी ।


रेशमको गुलाबी पटुकीले बाँधी बोकेकी छु
आँगमा,
आठ महिनाकी दूधे, मेरी सानी छोरी,
यो रोएको-रोयै छे च्याँट्टिएर—
मानौं मेरो व्यथा देख्छे
मानौं मेरो कष्ट भोग्छे
यसको पनि बिहे हुनेछ जब ।

## Books
Yukari Meldrum

For two years in grades five and six
I lacked the words to express
my sorrows at being bullied

Because I had no one to talk to
I went to the library where thousands of pages
offered me different worlds to live in

I'm forever grateful to those books
that kept my young life going

**Books** Tiffany Adair
Lithograph
2015

# Dream Journey

Yukari Meldrum


A huge bird scoops me up
high into the sky.
Having spent my whole life
low on the ground,
I'm fascinated
with the vastness —
the ever-changing colours.

As time passes,
I start to miss where I came from,
the solid ground where I can run
on my own two feet
without relying on the bird
to take me everywhere.

But the large bird has done
so much for me already,
I haven't the heart to say
I want to get back to the land
and walk on my own.
I know the bird would be sad
to see me go.

So, I stay in my life
in the grasp of the bird.

One day,
I cannot stand it any longer.
I need to escape.

I struggle, struggle, struggle.
The bird grips harder,
keeps me in its talons.

At last I yell at the bird,
*I don't need you anymore!*

The bird, astonished,
releases me.

Feeling the pains
of scratches and cuts
all over my body,
I fall through the sky —
freedom fresh in the air.

**Falling Through a Dream** Tiffany Adair
Lithograph
2015

# On a January Day

Yukari Meldrum

An unusually warm day
above the freezing point.
A ladybug appears out of the blue
sensing the long-awaited spring.

Nature doesn't seem to care.
Next day, it dips to minus thirty-five.
Ladybug falls into a sleep
from which she never wakens.

# Prairie Morning
Yukari Meldrum

The deep night blue as I get in the car
The sky gradually gleams lighter

Heading west against
the heavy traffic going downtown

The eastern horizon cracks open
in my rearview mirror

Just enough clouds to tint the sky
numerous shades of crimson

The snow-covered fields ahead
the pink grapefruit

The rising light peeks on the mirror
as red as a blood orange

I shift my gaze to the road, the pink gone
The fields shine silver as their normal selves

# Balance Challenged

Yukari Meldrum

Accustomed to walking
on the flat surfaces of the prairies
I stumble on the slope
as I climb and admire
the colors of row houses of St. John's

Not used to having sea winds
blowing on me at all times
I stumble on the rocks
when I hop hop over
to view a fishing boat at Petty Harbour

**Jumping, Twisting, Rolling, Searching** Tiffany Adair
Lithograph
2015

# A Gap
Yukari Meldrum


I help Nishat into my car
put her wheelchair in the trunk

A skinny, frail white woman approaches
asks if we can spare some change for bread and milk

I mumble excuses under my breath
get into the driver's seat, don't give her any

*What if I give her money?*
*Will she really use it for food?*

I pull out of the parking lot
Nishat bursts into red hot anger

    That woman walks on both of her legs
    speaks English as a native speaker
    wears a warm coat and leather boots

    Professionals from other countries
    clean people's houses, drive cabs—you know,
    tough and dirty jobs, anything they can get

She doesn't know how lucky she is
that she was born in this country

This woman who has to beg for money
I don't know what her problem might be

Nishat has been studying English
forever waiting for her immigration papers

*What can I say?*

# Single White Man

Yukari Meldrum

On a Saturday morning, he strolls by the Eiffel Tower
whose feet are dipped in a pool of tourists

he wonders why these people are attracted
to a building that's just a building, after all

he's got everything he ever wanted right here
in a city where everyone wants to be

lives in a home his grandparents gave him
without having to ask for it even once

he is the chosen one out of all his siblings
and everyone in the family knows it

works as a program producer for popular shows
and, naturally, girls always want a tour

he walks by a busy crowd of multi-colored people
who buzz and swarm in the most visited city

*why do I feel alone?*

# One, Two, Three, Four…
Yukari Meldrum


Visiting the country for the weekend,
I fed some barn cats outside.
Although they were not house cats,
they were friendly and happy
when I gave them food –
food to live on.

Next day, there were four cats instead of five.
Again the following day, only four cats.

Dogs were sticking their noses in
the small space under the shed.
The fifth cat with no name
stretched out alone
in the air below the freezing point.

The coldness of the cat
I had never felt before…
Underneath the thick fur
was icy cold flesh.

In the solid ground
I managed to dig a hole
to swallow up the frozen body
of the furry cat.

Warm tears down my cheeks,
never freezing.

**Unseeing Eyes** Tiffany Adair
Lithograph
2015

**TIFFANY ADAIR**

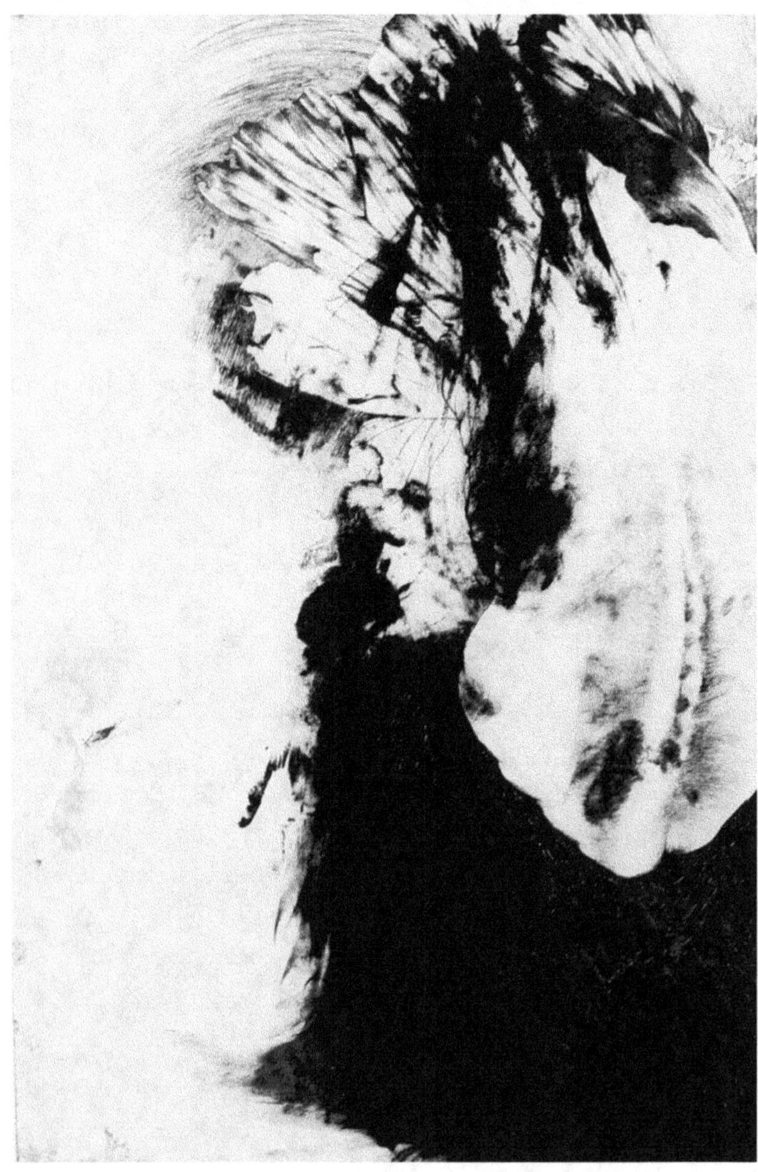

**A Marvellous Experiment** Tiffany Adair
Lithograph, chine collé
2014

# A Marvellous Experiment
Pushpa Raj Acharya

On this island,
my body has undergone
many marvelous experiments.

In this old tale,
a feather falls first
and then a horseman.

# Of Dead Plants and
# Shriveled Flowers

Yukari Meldrum

Why do memories
cause silent aches in my heart?
Even very tender ones –
never coming back again
simply traces of the past

**Of Dead Plants and Shriveled Flowers** Tiffany Adair
Lithograph, chine collé
2014

**Can I Fade Away Now?**
**(version 2)** Tiffany Adair
Lithograph, chine collé
2014

# Can I Fade Away Now?

Yukari Meldrum

When I finish learning
what I'm destined to
on this planet,
can I fade away forever?
Or, will I come back to life?

# Shadows

Sharmila Pokharel

The gods I bowed to,
the Himalayas I saw,
were only shadows.

I thought
sisters and brothers,
relatives and friends
and all those who walked beside me,
were humans;
but they, too, were only shadows.

Praises and prizes,
rounds of applause were
also shadows that vanished after sunset and
came back after sunrise.

My delusion was deep.

## She Eats
Pushpa Raj Acharya

Death is yet another name for love
Two are one, deep in the core

The softest breeze can slay me stiff
But I desire her love ever more

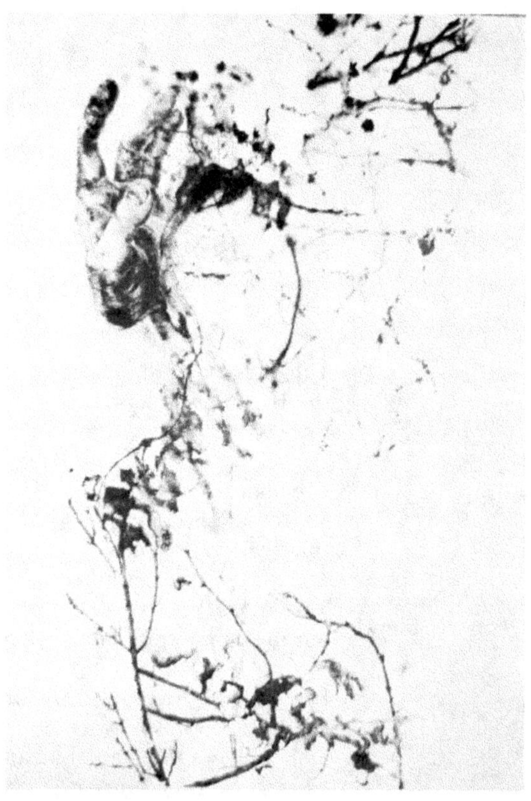

**She Eats** Tiffany Adair
Lithograph
2013

## Beauty
Sharmila Pokharel

Facial smoothness
changed into wrinkles

How could you ignore
the process of nature and time?

**Useless** Tiffany Adair
Lithograph, digital, chine collé
2014

## Dilemma
Sharmila Pokharel


Home:
I was just a drop of water,
but I assumed I was the ocean

Abroad:
After everything was flooded
by the tempest of time,
I was left alone on the bank

Still just a drop of water,
I try to converge
silently with the ocean,
but dried up as vapours

## Useless
Yukari Meldrum


You think it was
all for nothing
but you know
sometimes
what lingers on
is something
that appeared
useless
at the time

**To the Simplest Core of
the Matter** Tiffany Adair
Lithograph, digital, chine collé
2014

## To the Simplest Core
## of the Matter
Pushpa Raj Acharya


The strokes of cattle's hooves on dirt roads
create swirls of dust
that blend with the twilight rays of the golden sun.
The mélange forms a canvas where
an artist drops lines, curves, leaves.
Imagination is homecoming at its core.

## Silence
Sharmila Pokharel


Holding my chin in my right hand
watching yellow leaves
falling from trees

Busy mornings
crowded trains
but now and then, what
I have is silence

People in front of me
with white headphones
and black cell phones
I see them every day at the same time
but they look more unfamiliar
each time

Outside the train window,
long lines of cars
moving in rush
Pedestrians watching
for signal lights,
ready to cross

**Untitled (version 1)** Tiffany Adair
Lithograph
2014

**Untitled (version 2)** Tiffany Adair
Lithograph, chine collé
2014

## Untitled
Pushpa Raj Acharya

When I breathe
the wind swings the world
and whispers:
"Let me be in your dreams.
I have seen a life of joy,
now let me show it to you."

## Two
Yukari Meldrum

Where do I end, and
how do I know where you start?
How will I ever learn
where the boundary between
the two of us really exists?

# ARTIST BIOGRAPHIES

ARTIST BIOGRAPHIES

## TIFFANY ADAIR

**Tiffany Adair** was born, raised, and educated in Edmonton, Alberta, Canada. She graduated from the University of Alberta in 2014 with a Bachelor of Fine Arts Degree. Since then, she has won the International Sculpture Center's Outstanding Student Achievement in Contemporary Sculpture Award, was selected to participate in the Tokyo Screen Print Biennale, and continues to find ways to stay involved and active in the Edmonton arts scene. She is always looking for new and interesting ideas and collaborations to explore, and has been infected indefinitely by the travel bug.

## YUKARI MELDRUM

**Yukari Meldrum** is a Japanese–English Certified Translator (Canada) who also reads and writes whenever she feels like it. Words simply fascinate her. In addition, she finds that special space between the two languages and two cultures an intriguing place to be.

## PUSHPA RAJ ACHARYA

**Pushpa Raj Acharya** is a poet from Nepal. He travels between languages and landscape. He has collaborated with musicians, artists, community workers, and other poets. His first poetry book, *Chhayakal "The Phantom Time"* (FinePrint, Kathmandu, 2006) was in Nepali and the second one, *Dream Catcher* (Vajra Publications, Kathmandu, 2012) was in English.

## SHARMILA POKHAREL

**Sharmila Pokharel** was born in Nepal and immigrated to Canada in 2010. She is the author of three collections of poetry. Her latest work, *My Country in a Foreign Land: Paradeshmaa Mero Desh* is a bilingual poetry collection (co-translated by Alice Major). Her earlier books, *Astitwa Nariko, "Women's Existence"* (1997) and *Amiba ra Kuntiharu "Amoeba and Kuntis"* (2000) were in Nepali. She has received various prizes, including the Cultural Diversity in Arts Award in 2012.

www.ingramcontent.com/pod-product-compliance
Lightning Source LLC
Chambersburg PA
CBHW080524030726
47592CB00012B/3462